Materials Around Us

Written by Paul Mason
Illustrated by Clive Goodyer

T0385919

Look Around You

How many materials can you see here?

t—shirt

book

jug and cup

tyre swing

How are materials made?
Read this book to find out!

bin

cotton

rubber

paper

metal

glass

Cotton

Do you wear cotton like this boy?

Cotton comes from plants.

First it is made into thread.

The thread is made into cloth.

Then the cloth is made into clothes!

Rubber

Rubber is used to make toys, tools and boots.

Rubber comes from trees.

It drips from a spout that is put in the tree.

It is left to dry out.

Then it is made into flat sheets.

Glass

Glass is used to make windows, bowls and spectacles.

Glass is made from sand.

The sand is heated.

Then it melts.

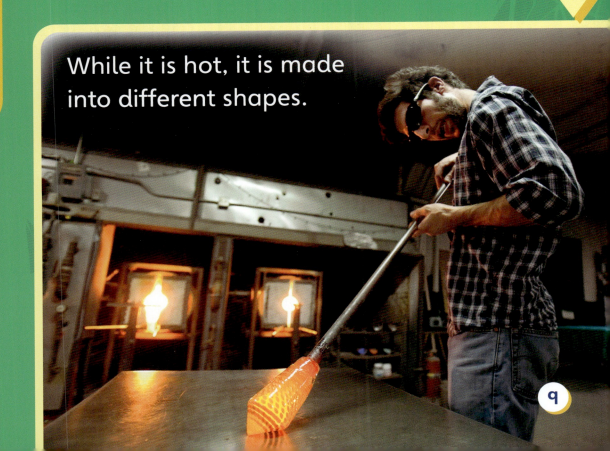

While it is hot, it is made into different shapes.

Paper

Paper is used for lots of different things. It can be used for drawing. Or you could make a paper hat!

Paper is made from trees.

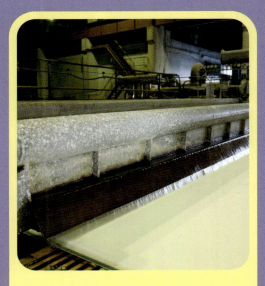

Wood is ground up into small bits.

Water is added to make a mushy pulp.

The pulp is dried to make paper.

Metal

Metal is used to make toys and coins, slides and steering wheels.

Metal is made from rocks that have been broken up.

The rocks are heated.

Then they are cooled.

This makes the metal.

Recycling

All of these materials can be used again.

Using old materials to make new things is called recycling.

Here are some things that can be made from materials that have been recycled.

Old newspaper can be made into toilet roll.

Old glass bottles can be made into marbles.

Old metal cans can be made into new cans.

Index

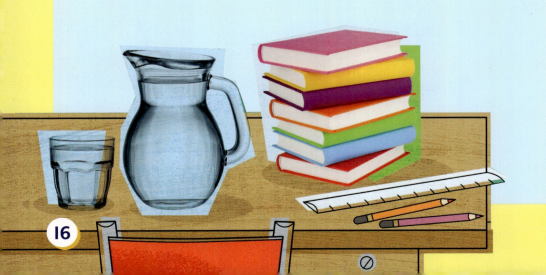